KEEPING THE
SERVANT SPARK

KEEPING THE SERVANT SPARK

Encouragement For Christian Caregivers

ARNOLD KUNTZ

Publishing House
St. Louis

Copyright © 1992 Concordia Publishing House
3558 S. Jefferson Avenue, St. Louis, MO 63118-3968
Manufactured in the United States of America

Library of Congress Cataloging-in-Publication Data.

Kuntz, Arnold G., 1926–
    Keeping the Servant Spark/Arnold G. Kuntz
    ISBN 0-570-04562-2
    1. Church work—Lutheran Church.   I. Title.
BV4400.K86 1992
248.8'92—dc20   91-29935
                                          CIP

1 2 3 4 5 6 7 8 9 10   01 00 99 98 97 96 95 94 93 92

Contents

How to Use This Book

This book is written for all caring Christians, be they church professionals or lay people. It can be used in at least two ways—for personal reflective reading, and for group discussion.

At minimum this volume can give support to the caring person in ministry—to enhance, to challenge, to give care to the caregiver. This book can also provide a group of caregivers a vehicle to discuss the issues that each chapter brings out. Through group discussion that emphasizes the Gospel, both personal growth and team building can occur.

Dr. Kenneth C. Haugk, Director of the Stephen Series system of lay caring ministry, has written the five questions at the end of each chapter. Your group may cover all five or select from among them. What you decide to do depends on the particular interests of the group members as well as the time you wish to devote to discussion.

There are also some steps or activities so you can go farther into the issue and subject, as well as a closing prayer.

Whether you read this book individually or in combination with a group of other caregivers, may this be a growth-producing experience for you and for all those you serve. God bless your life and ministry!

Preface

If what follows comes off sounding like nothing more than ordinary, common, Christian advice for ordinary, common, Christian people, that's because I see church workers, most of them anyway, as ordinary, common, Christian folks trying desperately to keep keel to the current in a particularly turbulent and rocky stretch of the river. People who work in the church in one capacity or other, professionals and volunteers alike, aren't, as far I can tell, that much different from other people. Their jobs are unique; their responsibilities are exceptional; their "calling," as baptized people, dying and rising with Christ, is from out of this world. But they themselves are just folks, and from time to time they need fresh motivation and a renewed spirit of perseverence.

At any rate, what we have to say, as far as the basics are concerned, is quite as apropos for any church member, as it is for pastors and so-called "professionals" in the church and its active leaders. So if you who have never felt God lay his hand on you at the altar of ordination want to peek over our shoulder or cock an ear to what follows, welcome!

What follows pretty well defies the rules of outline. If one chapter relates to another, it's more a matter of happenstance than logic. I've simply set out some notions as they occurred, and that is a process which, after long years of habit, tends to be pretty haphazard. If you live and serve long enough in church circles, a few ideas are likely to surface on the subject of "church work." I've related them just the way they came to mind. So, fellow pastor, teacher, DCE—colleagues all—partners, church leaders, and good old "you can always count on me" volunteers, for what it's worth, here is a thought or two for you, to help keep your servant spark alive.

Arnold G. Kuntz

Chapter 1

A Sane Self-Estimate

Whoever wants to become great among you
must be your servant, and whoever wants to
be first must be slave of all. For even the Son
of Man did not come to be served, but to serve,
and to give his life as a ransom for many.
Mark 10:43–45:

Once upon a time in a far-away land, there was a no-nonsense, authoritative, powerhouse church leader who was, to all intents and purposes, nearly perfect. Three weeks into this person's career as a recognized worker in the church, God convened a high-level meeting of administrative angels in heaven, and it was decided—unanimously—never to let that happen again. That was, on the face of it and in its profoundest sense, a good move on God's part. For one thing, there are very few nearly perfect people from whom to draw workers for the church; and for another, nearly perfect people are, by and large and almost by definition, mostly certified pains in the neck.

The high-level decision more often than not to settle upon patently average to mediocre people to comprise the work corps of Christendom has not, however, totally solved a besetting problem for the church militant. Even among those of us who are rather patently average human beings, a significant number regard themselves as nearly perfect, or at least feel the need to purport themselves as such. All too often this creates among those for whom church workers, professionals and volunteers, labor and toil, the same kind of subcranial distress which is produced by actual near perfection. It's a problem we ought to address, and will. However, for

11

now, to begin with, let's all take some comfort from the knowledge that it is part of God's purpose and design to employ the manifestly imperfect as "laborers in the vineyard."

This notion—that church workers are well advised not to think of themselves "more highly than they ought"—is not a new or novel idea at all. It occurred to God initially one day as he cast about in the Garden of Eden looking for Adam and found him naked and frightened, as was the woman with him. God was astounded to discover that they had invented a whole new concept called "fig leaf survival." For Adam, the idea that he might really not be the hotshot he presumed to be was driven home to him as he looked analytically at his wife and concluded, "The woman, whom, come to think of it, *God* gave me, leaves a thing or two to be desired in the area of obedience."

But God would not let Adam pin the blame for his own disobedience on either Eve or her Creator. And since Adam and Eve are a sort of generic representation of the people who follow in their train, it was reasonable to assume that all their descendants would have their less-than-perfect moments too. Having recognized their own imperfection, a fig leaf or two, they concluded, was called for to "cover up," as the saying goes.

St. Paul, under the pressure of inspiration, got the point as well, suggesting there is value in taking a long look in the mirror to discover that the old self ("the old Adam" was his phrase for it) had best not be regarded as a paragon of virtue, worth, or excellence (Eph. 4:22). You don't have to invest much time ("brief but regular" and "repeated" are key phrases when it comes to the exercise of self-contemplation), and you don't have to probe very deeply, to discover that imperfections, deficiencies, and downright iniquities outnumber by a wide margin any good in us.

The trouble is, no sooner do you pin down what's wrong with you, and a little voice within reminds you that, for all of that, you are considerably better than a lot of people you know. You are careful in your language, respectful of the elderly, and patient to the point of being long-suffering. Besides, being occupied, for the most part, by matters churchly ought to count for something. Think of all the sacrifices you are making for God's sake, doing a lot of things down at the church which nobody even knows about or, if they do, they fail to appreciate. Some of you even "fast twice a week and give tithes of all that you possess."

King David, (2 Sam. 12:13), Simon Peter (Luke 5:8), and the prodigal son (Luke 15:18) began their roads to effectiveness on their knees in confession. Simply put, there is no route to successful service in the church which does not originate in the daily practice of self-assessment, because the knowledge we have of ourselves discourages harboring too lofty an opinion of ourselves. There's an old Lenten hymn which asks rather pointedly, "Would He devote that sacred head for such a worm as I?" Worm, indeed. But with the years I'm beginning to understand what Isaac Watts had in mind. You can't grow older before the face of Jesus and in the light of his love without sinking in your own esteem, not if you think honestly about Jesus' goodness and your lack of it.

So, when all is said and done, with a little honest reflection we ought to arrive at the point where we can shed that stuffy, pompous baggage which turns off so many when they come face-to-face with the workers of the church. Nonetheless, a word of caution is in order here. It's one thing to be just plain folks, one of the gang, an ordinary person; and quite another to wallow in the muddy gutters of worldliness. Mud wallowing fails to think highly enough of our work in the church or of ourselves as we work for her. It's as much a mistake to underrate ourselves.

In our modern world we've developed some expertise for mud wallowing as well. Who are you, after all? What difference do you make? What can you do about anything? Who's going to be any better off for anything you do? I don't know. I can't answer that question. Not that any number of people couldn't be better off for what you do. That's the secret, of course. If you look down on your job, your position, what

Luther calls "your station in life," and regard it of small importance, you'll usually find you aren't using it to anybody's advantage but your own, and that, to tell you the truth, *isn't* important. But if you perceive each new day to be a full slice of life to be fashioned after the manner that God has decreed, I don't think it will seem small or insignificant to you.

The Bible in verse after verse makes you feel totally bankrupt (Ps. 40:12; Eccl. 9:3; Ps. 14:2-3; Jer. 16:12; Mk. 7:21). But the Bible has another side to it—the dominant side, the ultimate side—which smiles on us and cradles us and sets us down among the stars and calls us "chosen instruments" (Acts 9:15).

This is the eternal paradox of Christian ministry. It all begins on your knees with the self-assessment of Martin Luther, "a lost and condemned creature," but rises up then on the wings of each morning until I am "His own, and live under Him in his kingdom, and serve Him in everlasting righteousness, innocence, and blessedness." You are nobody, and so am I, except God's messenger—that's the truth! We are nothing, I'd agree with that, except his "candlesticks!" Those who fail to keep these two extremes in everlasting tension, not thinking more highly of themselves than they ought, yet not underrating the task or the calling either, will find the rigors of working in the church quite beyond them.

For Group or Personal Reflection

1. Do you ever think that you are perfect or almost perfect? What does it do to you at those times? What does it do to others?
2. Do you know anyone who comes across as perfect, at least some of the time? How do you feel about that person? How do you think that person feels about himself? How can you show compassion to that individual, and perhaps even help him or her?
3. What is one way that you are imperfect?
4. What is one imperfection that you are working to change? How is it going?

5. How does God work with our imperfections to make us even better servants? Be specific.

To Take This One Step Farther

1. List three of your habits which make you less than a perfect fit for work in the kingdom.
2. List three elements of your service or ministry which elevate your work above the ordinary.

Prayer

Son of the living God, and yet, for all of that, companion, brother, friend, I am humbled by your grace and goodness in choosing to become my confidant and letting me become your coworker. Help me balance humility with appropriate pride in a way that befits a sinner who has become a craftsman in your kingdom by your great grace and generosity. I bring this one thing to you for forgiving and for cleansing: my penchant for _____.

I am your child. I serve your people. Make me worthy, by your mercy. Make me upright, by your power. Amen.

Chapter 2

Sweet Reasonableness

All of you, clothe yourselves with humility toward one another, because, "God opposes the proud but gives grace to the humble." Humble yourselves, therefore, under God's mighty hand, that he may lift you up in due time. 1 Pet. 5:5–6

What we talked about in chapter one is realism. What we're talking about now is humility. There's a difference. You can take a full, hard look at yourself and draw the conclusion that you are still a long, sea mile from perfection. That's realism. Humility is something else again. Humility is a hallmark of the renewed spirit. It is a Christian trait (Matt. 11:29), a holy skill (Matt. 18:4). Matthew Arnold calls it "sweet reasonableness" and, in Greek ethics, humility describes the one who "doesn't press for the last farthing of his rights." Smart people, those Greeks.

Humility exercises constant deference; it is instantly and abidingly concerned for the other fellow, selfless. Modern psychology can't take it in large doses and tends to believe its self-denying aspects bring on severe headaches over the eyes and gastronomic distress. Actually, lack of humility causes heartburn, along with a whole catalogue of human complaints. "If," you fret and worry, "I don't take care of #1, who will?" Humility doesn't have any such preoccupation. It's not concerned about #1, since it has turned that anxiety over to God.

Humility is a difficult thing to explain since there is so little of it around to point to for an example. King Saul had it early on (1 Sam. 9:21), though in his case, as with so many of us, it was a fleeting thing, and in the end pride did him in. The centurion in Matthew 8 demonstrated a flash of it. Jesus is the best example, humbling himself and becoming obedient to the point of death.

For our purpose, I propose a visit with John the Baptizer to throw some light on the subject. John is best known, of course, for having declared, "He (Christ) must become greater, I must become less," or more familiarly in the King James version, "He must increase; I must decrease," which is the way it goes for the humble.

John did many more things in life—remarkable things—besides coming up with a quotable syllogism on humility. He was, don't forget, the phenom of his day, orator extraordinaire, spell-binder. "The whole Judean countryside and all the people of Jerusalem went out to him" (Mark 1:5). As one pretty fair country preacher some years ago has pointed out, John did not have to announce sensational, topical subjects, or themes flavored with a dash of politics. He didn't find it necessary to promise brief, bright services with a short homily and the rest all hearty music. The people were not coaxed or cajoled. They just came—soldiers, theologians, commoners, doctors of divinity, professors, and the scientific intelligentsia of the day. But who remembers John's considerable accomplishments? What we recall is that he said, "He must increase; I must decrease." Ho-hum.

It must have been even more difficult for John to say that than it is for us. For his career John had given up everything—comfort, security, human love. Who hasn't, of course? Not everything, maybe. Not human love, really, and modern medical plans and pensions offer some security. But just imagine what might be yours today if you had devoted your focus and your gifts to the world of commerce or medicine instead of to the church.

And John had the crowds in the palm of his hand. They were his. He had built up his congregation from scratch. It was as if he had married them, baptized their offspring, sweated it out in the hospital waiting room with them late at night, and buried their dead. They were his, his congregation. Give it all over to Christ? Just like that? Knowing that once gone, they were gone for good? And some of them were his closest friends, his most dependable aides, such as John the beloved and Andrew. Do you think maybe he muttered a little when he made out their transfer, or took it personally when they left—family and all—to join the crowds around Jesus? Did he grit his teeth when he said, "He must increase; I must decrease?" I don't think so.

John had the rare, great grace to understand it doesn't really matter who does the work so long as the work gets done. His attitude in effect reasoned, "How much does John the Baptist count since God gets the credit? Who cares about the messenger if the message gets through?" John had what is called humility. He wasn't focused on himself. He wasn't concerned with getting the credit. Let John be forgotten. "*He must increase.*"

God bless John the Baptist, and may he teach us too. Our Christian service has a way of getting all mixed up with precedence. Church workers grow sensitive about personal things. When others supersede us or fail to consult us sufficiently, we mutter under our breath or belittle our rival's achievements.

What was John's secret? It starts, and probably ends there too, with his relationship with God. He was rooted, as the old farm folk saw it, in God. To have your roots wound round the rock that is our God is the most steadying thing in all the world. It gives you a place for your feet when the bottom is falling out, a certainty that whatever happens or doesn't, however lightly you are held, however totally you are ignored, there is a most knowledgeable, understanding heart in control. If you do the noble thing, the unselfish thing, that heart, that rock, that God will not finally let you down.

Besides, John knew he stood with everybody else on the sinners' side of the line. John saw in Jesus a greatness he himself did not possess, alongside of which he faded into insignificance. Church workers would do well to remember

Jesus once a day, and stand in his presence for a few moments when the work begins each morning or (better: and) when they're turning out the lights at night. We'd all be in for a surprise to discover how such a simple exercise causes our sore thumbs, our snubbed feelings, even our bitter disappointments, to shrink to truer proportions.

On some frayed and yellowed page somewhere I once found these words:

O the bitter shame and sorrow,
All of self and none of Thee.

Yet You found me, I beheld You.
Some of self and some of Thee.

Day by day Thy tender mercy.
Less of self and more of Thee.

Higher than the highest heavens.
None of self and all of Thee.

For Group or Personal Reflection
1. What are the struggles you have with humility?
2. How can genuine humility be reconciled with healthy self-esteem?
3. How can humility be game playing, perhaps even manipulative?
4. When is it the right time to defer to others?
5. When is it the right thing to defer to others?

To Take This One Step Farther
1. List three persons to whom you will consciously defer this week.
2. Choose one item of ministry, perhaps some "deed of kindness done," which you will keep secret from everyone. Keep it solely to yourself, and consider no credit due, just service rendered.

Prayer

Help me, Lord, be good for nothing in my own right; make me a laborer in your kingdom of grace, not for what I can get out of it but for what I can put into it. No one, and I least of all, can outgive your unsparing liberality. Make it my purpose to exalt your name and serve my fellow humans without reference to those benefactions which you lavish on your servants. Not for that which I may get but for what I have already gotten in Christ, I would work for you and for your church. Amen.

Chapter 3

Accentuate the Positive

Give thanks in all circumstances, for this is God's will for you in Christ Jesus. 1 Thess. 5:18

A recent edition of a highly regarded West Coast newspaper uscd the words "critics" and "critical" four times on the first three pages. And that was only in the headlines. Anybody with an ear to the ground and one eye on the television set knows that "finding fault" describes a modern way of life, *the* modern way of life. Nowadays it is regarded appropriate, even essential, to "fix the blame." Whether it's apartheid in South Africa or the dwindling population of lady bugs in the Los Angeles basin, somebody has to be nailed. It's an interesting philosophy with roots, really, in the notion "I've got rights, you know." Focus on that idea long enough, especially if you perceive that yours are being infringed upon, and you are bound inevitably to conclude, "And you've got wrongs!"

Some very successful (at least lucrative) professions have flowered in the arbors of reproval. Consumer advocates invest the lion's share of time and effort in cataloging what is wrong with everything from the way farmers grow beets, to the deficiencies of pharmaceutical regulation. The new age of litigation builds its house on the premise that somebody somewhere is to blame—for something, for everything.

Alas, the injunction of Scripture notwithstanding, "in the world" often means "of the world"; so the church has its full compliment of fault-finders too. Not that we had to learn much from the world that we hadn't already mastered by doing what comes naturally!

Already in the wilderness of what is now Saudi Arabia in

23

the fifteenth century B.C., there was a whole congregation of God's people laying its complaint at Moses' doorstep. "If only we had died by the Lord's hand in Egypt," they said. "There we sat around pots of meat and ate all the food we wanted" (Ex. 16:3). The Pharisees, church members elite in Jesus' day, were all over Jesus for keeping unacceptable company (Luke 15:2). At least church people in the good old days had the grace to keep their faultfinding and blame fixing to a low mutter. "Murmur" is the Biblical word for it.

Today it's right out there in the open, loud and clear, and well regarded as if it were one's solemn duty and contribution to church life, health, and welfare. You won't have to look far into your own experience to isolate this person or that whose total input to the daily commerce of Christian history is to tell you what's wrong and, likely as not, how your own failures and shortcomings have contributed to the break-down. If you ask innocently enough what he or she plans to do about repairing the wrong, the look you get begins at utter bafflement and moves in successive stages until it arrives at haughty disgust. Do? They already did. They have told you and anybody else who would listen what's wrong. That's their part, don't you see? That's it, and there are plenty to join them, and thus, they must suppose, they "fulfill the law of Christ."

If I were going to write an essay for ordinary, run-of-the-mill church members, I'd lay it on heavy right here. But this is a word to the caregivers of the church, the professionals and the lay leaders and the volunteers who have taken upon themselves to get out in front and lead the parade—the standard setters. So what I'd like to do, under the circumstances, is lay it on heavy right here.

Finding what is wrong and fixing the blame for it is all too often a primary activity for church workers, too. Set aside fifteen minutes of your next church workers' conference, or, more locally, your weekly caregivers' group or the bimonthly meeting of the church council, simply to listen. I can almost guarantee you will be educated on everything from the senior pastor's atrocious work habits to the total mismanagement of denominational pension funds.

When church workers allow themselves the luxury of faultfinding and blame-fixing in the presence of the "dear hearts and gentle people" who live and move on their home turf, this is leadership at its most effectively destructive level because it honors negativism with the good church seal of approval. It opens the floodgate to a rush of "bad blabbing," all of which limits somebody's ministry, minimizes somebody's efforts, narrows somebody's sphere of effectiveness, and drags the church down to the level of our modern world at its worst. Beware! The victim, when all is said and done, might well be you, and while I'd never want to say it, that might be justice at its most poetic.

Try something. Now. Right there under your reading lamp or on the commuter bus or wherever you are reading this at the moment. Think of one good thing you can say for your denomination—just one—or for your senior pastor, the members of your congregation, or Billy Graham. Got it? Now, as quickly as you can find the opportunity for it, tell that one thing to someone. Did that little exercise make you feel good? It does require a little extra effort. Anybody can find and tell what's wrong. But you have done the unique, the special thing. You found and said something good. Whatever it was, it was designed to expand, to maximize, to abet and bless somebody's influence. That's got to feel good.

What you may not appreciate is that you have begun to set a pattern which, at the very least, will cause people to pause, to hesitate to engage in "bad mouthing" in your presence, or to heckle and complain. Who's going to whisper out of the side of his mouth to you if he knows from experience that you are forever finding the good, picking out the positive, and beaming as if the victory is won, as if God's Christians are precious and chosen, as if in the back of your head is a melody of praise and happy adoration? If you are spared someone else's daily review of negatives and his personal book of lamentations, you might well cancel your pending appointment with your local psychiatrist and invest all the time you are saving in securing the next available tee time and/or let go with a bar or two of "Glory Be To Jesus."

How long would you suppose a sales person for Mary Kay cosmetics would keep her job if her sales pitch included: (a) a systematic review of her products' shortcomings and failures; (b) the complaint that the home office and its operation ought to reorganize after the pattern of Estee Lauder and Company; and, (c) the verdict that the raspberry glace' lipstick has a tendency to make your complexion appear pale and sickly? Not long.

Of course, the church does not fire its professional detractors. Yet it might respectfully remind them that there is a time and place for constructive criticism. But there are other times and there are other places where such criticism is devastating, where it can minimize the effectiveness of Christ's church. It can dull the edge; it can erode and finally extinguish altogether a soul's ardor for Christ. So—cut that out. With all the good things you can focus on, from the grace of God in Christ to last Sunday's brave attempt on the part of the youth choir to render "For All The Saints," that you should let pass your lips the denigrating word! Give thanks. Rejoice ... always. Be happy. Shout. Sing. Clap your hands, and, above all, praise God from whom all blessings flow.

For Group or Personal Reflection
1. When is criticism destructive?
2. When is criticism beneficial?
3. What does constant negative criticism do to the criticizer?—the criticized?
4. Was Jesus ever critical? If so, when? Why?
5. What is one thing you are critical of right now in your life?—in the church? What are you personally going to do to help the situation?

To Take This One Step Farther
1. List five good work-related things to say before the day is out. Practice saying them.

2. Say them to someone, somewhere.
3. Assess their effect on the ones with whom you shared them, and on you.

Prayer

> Savior, fix my eyes on what is right and good and helpful. You desire us to eliminate all that minimizes the efforts of your people. Make my words good words, my thoughts helpful thoughts and all my deeds such as build up and make the most of your church on earth. Let all that comes from me and goes through me be to the praise and glory of the Father in the highest heaven. Amen.

Chapter 4

God's Messengers of Peace

For we preach not ourselves, but Jesus Christ the Lord, and ourselves as your servants for Jesus' sake. 2 Cor. 4:5

A funeral is, I guess, as good a place as any for conceiving an idea. But this was a flash of total revelation, a full-blown concept with all its parts. It caught my mental eye and commanded my attention. And all this right in the middle of the pastor's funeral homily. "If," a voice within me kept repeating, "you want to observe Christian pastors at their very best, observe them as they conduct the funerals for their good members." The most mediocre somehow attain nobler heights and demonstrate greater ability when conducting a funeral. The worst drum majors shed their pomposity when they are pastoring via an "earth to earth" committal. Certainly the person I was observing as he ministered to the bereaved on a stifling summer afternoon was superb.

Several things contribute to that phenomenon. For one thing the subject, the central thought under consideration, is victory, a patently more positive theme than sin, law, or the annual budget. Not human victory, not in the first place, though the entire point is that it can, by grace through faith, become ours. And not just the deceased's either, our dear departed friend now fallen asleep, though a pastor at a funeral is leading the celebration because victory is now his. It's the victory of Christ himself upon which the pastor is focused. With a theme and a focus like that, the most ordinary clergy inevitably operate on high ground. For the same reason, on

Easter Sunday run-of-the-mill preachers come off sounding like Billy Sunday or St. Francis of Assisi.

The point is, church workers are at their best when they move very close to the heartbeat of the Christian faith. You may bring off a victory or two by reason of your considerable abilities in discussions concerning next year's budget or organizing next month's youth-sponsored car wash. But you can't miss if you make your point of contact the everlasting victory of Jesus Christ.

One of the nicest compliments I ever received came from a hard-to-please matron who said, "For all that (a phrase by which was intended to embrace a whole spectrum of inabilities too enormous to catalogue), no matter what the question, you do come up with helpful answers." What that lady was unaware of was a bit of advice an old pastor had shared with me when he was instructing me in the fine art of Bible class teaching. "No matter what question you are asked," he told me, "go cross country just as fast as your legs will carry you to the cross. Then, from there, whatever you offer will have value." The cross and the empty tomb: keep them in mind, in the front of your mind. They advance by many a factor the quality of what we do.

Another contributing factor to that pastor's remarkable funeral ministry I observed was the obvious fact that he cared. It's easy to care at a funeral. Caring not only improves our work in the church and elevates it, it becomes the unmistakable mark of a good church worker. The thing is, it's easier to care, to show care, at a funeral—a whole lot easier—than it is to show care at a committee meeting focused upon travel arrangements for the senior citizens' outing at the city park band concert next Thursday. Who cares? That's the point. Caring is the point. At that funeral the pastor cared. He cared for those to whom he ministered.

I recall a seminary professor who would climb up onto the desk at the front of the classroom, cross one leg over the other, deftly interlace the fingers of both hands and with a beatific grin declare, "You've got to be *for* people." All that just to declare, "You've got to be for people." That professor has died and gone to heaven, but the echo of his words and the memory of the way he underscored them lives on, at least in my heart. "You've got to be for people." Jesus cared when confronted by the hungry multitude (Matt. 14), or when accepting with good grace the sisters' gentle chiding, "If only you had been here . . ." and then calling Lazarus back for them (John 11), or commiserating with that outside-the-loop centurion whose servant was "grievously ill" (Matt. 8). And people whose hearts are filled with Jesus care.

Just one more thing. At a funeral people let pastors be what they are. At a funeral people perceive the pastor as pastor. Isn't there something to be learned at this point for all church workers? As long as this earth continues its spin through space, church workers will struggle beneath the heavy hand of purely illogical and totally inappropriate expectations on the part of those they serve. A three-week paid vacation is probably the most effective release there is from that phenomenon. But it is to the advantage of church workers (as well as their congregations) to maneuver as best they can into a posture which lets them freely be, and remind people that they are, the instruments of Jesus Christ, his candlesticks, with a message from heaven. What they really are about is rescue and hope, even when they're organizing the cleanup after the spaghetti dinner.

I've read a book or two about church marketing. Some of what they say is very good. All of it is better in your hands if you remember who you are, and what you are. If nothing else, when the sun goes down and the lights go out, you would do well to "lay me down to sleep" with the knowledge that for one more day you and yours have taken a few more steps in the march of victory. The souls in your keeping and the tables where you serve, God bless every one of them, are better off for what you've done, even if they don't see it. When all is said and done, you are at day's end God's messenger of peace. And that's a step toward restful sleep, indeed.

For Group or Personal Reflection

1. When are those times that bring out your ability to care the most?
2. When are those times that you most need care?
3. How is God in Christ involved in your caregiving?
4. Funerals celebrate the victory of Christ. At what other times do you particularly celebrate the victory of Christ?
5. During the more mundane times of life, how might you also celebrate the victory of Christ?

To Take This One Step Farther

1. Write out the central theme—the basic thought—of your personal ministry for the Lord Jesus.
2. Identify three instances today when you articulated that theme.
3. How do less obvious spiritual activities of your ministry serve to accomplish the theme of your ministry?

Prayer

> Author of inner peace, creator of all serenity of heart, my life and the lives of all with whom I live are marked by turmoil and upheaval and fear. You, and you alone, afford repose and provide quiet in the midst of life's turbulence and raging. Make me a messenger of peace. Cause me to declare and share the safety of soul which you bestow on all who trust in you. Amen.

Chapter 5

Pass the Buck to God

We know that in all things God works for the good of those who love him, who have been called according to his purpose. Rom. 8:28

There is no end to the catalogue of good things to be had by reading the Bible with diligence. High on the list is the fact that there is a whole host of helpful discoveries, particularly for church professionals and volunteer workers, which surfaces for the one who regularly opens his or her mind to the Spirit's moving by way of the pages of what the old venerables used to term "holy writ." Some of those discoveries are of great practical value for those who toil daily in the vineyards of the true and triune God.

For example, in Jer. 12:1 you come upon the remarkable revelation that the buck does not necessarily have to stop at your desk. The next time you find yourself staring blankly out the window or chewing on your eraser feeling sorry for yourself, pondering the machinations which have you forever to blame for everything from the summer slump to lagging contributions (synonyms from the treasurer's perspective), or responsible that Sunday School enrollment has fallen off by 13 percentage points since April, never suppose when it comes to your desk that the complaint—the reproach, whatever it is—has gone as far as it can go.

Instead of that, pull the Scriptures from the shelf, ferret out the Old Testament, Jeremiah in particular. Focus on chapter 12. Put your finger on verse one. Then watch the Monday blues disintegrate. Tuesday will become not just another hard day at the office. There it is: an escape, a way out. You too can do some buck-passing. You can get the monkey off your back, whatever it is. See how Jeremiah managed. He laid things at God's feet. He took the initiative and became assertive himself. "Let's consider for a moment your idea of justice, Lord. I'd like to know why. Why do the wicked prosper? Why do the righteous go without reward?"

Of course, in Jeremiah's case they were quite literally after his skin and not just in a manner of speaking. What's more, they had come terrifyingly close to turning the trick. It was at the hands of his own relatives that he had come dangerously close to losing his life. "Blood," someone has said, "is thicker than water, but it is still thin enough to spill," and Jeremiah's kin were quite intent on spilling his. So this much can be said for Jeremiah: he had a right to complain. He was not hollering before he had been hurt. That, it seems to me, is a thought which ought to give us pause.

Some of us are quite apt to sink into a blue funk over slights which are more imagined than real, or to bend under burdens which, looked upon with some perspective, might well be considered "our reasonable service." Maybe if we reviewed with a little discernment the "load we bear," we could quite simply eradicate half the things that weigh us down by the simple expedient of regarding them as blessings, privileges, and opportunities, rather than annoyances.

But with Jeremiah the problem was real enough. He had somehow gotten in way over his head, and quite innocently too, just doing what he thought he should. Notice then how he puts the finger on God. Oh, he starts out politely enough: "You are always righteous, Lord, when I bring a case before you." But we've all been in the business long enough to know what that kind of introduction augurs. "You're a nice enough person, John, but ..." "As deaconesses go, you're not nearly the problem they have at St. Over There. Nevertheless ... " Jeremiah, too: "You are righteous, of course, when I complain, yet ..." How is it, he wants to know, that sinners prosper and good people go without reward? There is enough in that for most of us to identify with him. There is something basically unfair about the fact that the harder I try, the more I get it in the neck. Others, who care so little, at the same time go along as if life were a stroll in the park.

Since Jeremiah's complaint puts in a nutshell the way we see it too, we'd best be ready to share with Jeremiah God's response when Jeremiah passes the buck. You will hardly believe it. It isn't what Jeremiah was looking for, or what we are. Instead of sympathy, he gets a word of challenge. Instead of soft words and comfortable clucking about the inherent toughness of life in this world with unique perplexities reserved for people who are particularly active in the church, you get this sort of rough, good-humored jollying: "You think what you've been going through is bad? Wait 'till you see what's coming. If what you've been facing gets you down, how will you be able to cope with what is waiting? If you have run with men, and that left you exhausted, how will you compete with horses? If you lose your footing in the relatively safe countryside, how will you make out in the ruggedness of Jordan?" (Jer. 12: 5).

That was not, no doubt, what Jeremiah wanted or expected to hear, and it probably set him back on his heels. It was, however, what Jeremiah needed to hear. If he could hang on while his country cousins pushed him around, his grip would be strong enough to hold him when the full force of officialdom came down on him. Each crisis prepares us for the next.

Church work is not a picnic in the park or a weekend in the country. If your labor among knowledgeable and committed Christians leaves you exhausted, disillusioned, and blue, how are you going to manage when you stand as God's deputy on the cutting edge in the struggle against devil, world, and flesh?

There are muscles in the Christian soul, and in their development practice makes perfect. It takes more than a stiff upper lip and a whistle in the dark to work in the church. You'll need the daily recollection that Jesus walks with you, your hand secure in his, through the valleys of shadows in your work and life, no matter where the path may lead. The Bible tells you it is so, but the daily experience secures us in the knowledge of it.

So every time you go through another "slough of despair," blame it on God. He's getting you ready for the next one, and the next one after that, until you can handle it blindfolded with one hand tied behind your back. Talk to somebody who's been around for a while, who's been active in the church for many a year. Look into his or her eyes. Maybe it doesn't get easier, but it does become more and more possible, as you develop the pattern of your walk with Jesus.

When you feel lonely and a little blue, pass the buck to God. Ask him, "What on earth is going on? My best efforts go for nothing while your enemies succeed." He'll likely tell you, "Never mind. If anything, it could get worse. Look how they treated my own Son. They'll treat you the same way. But remember how I treated him afterward."

For Group or Personal Reflection

1. What specific part or parts of the Bible have given you most strength?
2. Is it sometimes hard to *really* "pass the buck" to God? Share why that might be.
3. What are some of those things that particularly get you down? What have you done in those instances?
4. What loads do you bear that you actually might not need to bear?
5. Have you ever questioned God? Explain one or more of those times. How did God answer you? What was your response to God's answer?

To Take This One Step Farther

1. Look back across the years. Name your past hard experiences that have contributed to the caliber of your ministry and the strength of your character.
2. List from your memory three Bible characters for whom difficult times proved to be a blessing.

Prayer

I am content, O Father in heaven, to lay my
life in your hands. I am satisfied to entrust
to you the causes of truth and justice. I know
I can perceive but a feeble shadow of your
good purposes. To you, then, be the glory
and to me the comfort that you are in your
heavens doing precisely as you please. Because of Jesus I pray trustingly. Amen.

Chapter Six

A God Who Is Real

*Since we live by the Spirit, let us keep in step
with the Spirit.* Gal. 5:25

"Nobody is closer to God in this life than those who hate and
deny him." Martin Luther said that or, at the very least, words
to that effect. If you expect to get by with that sort of blatant
statement, it helps to be someone like Luther. That popped
out of his mouth after it welled up in an emotional moment
in his heart. Nevertheless, behind it was a very settled notion
in his mind, the result of a lot of sober consideration. At least
the one who denies God, Luther is suggesting, is taking the
idea of God seriously. He may be denying God, but he is not
insinuating that the idea of God is unimportant. He is not
taking God for granted.

Unless God matters to you totally, he doesn't really matter
to you. Unless your life in Christ demands you lay everything
on the line for him, it doesn't warrant the badge of Christian
life at all. Christianity is not another attachment like the Re-
publican party, the Rotary or the D.A.R. You hear a lot about
apathy and indifference in Christian circles, but few would
regard it to be worse than unbelief. Luther did. So does the
Bible. If you want a vivid assessment of how God feels about
apathy, read Rev. 3:16.

There are any number of forks in the road which we could
follow at this point. However, I intend to make this an appeal
to you to place the God of grace at the center of your daily
doings. It isn't enough to put God in his place—not when
that place is somewhere in the margins of your activities. It
is not enough to afford God an honorable position in your
existence, even an eminent one, if the Lord remains mean-

ingless to the things you do on Tuesdays and Thursdays. The person who surrounds God with candles and stained glass—who gives him a room, however properly appointed that opens only in the A.M. on Sundays—is not nearly so close to God as the unbeliever, the denier, since he isn't serious about God.

Could this have anything at all to do with you? Let's make the point. Beware of conventional piety. How much of our churchgoing is only habit? How often are our efforts to be kind and our attempts to be generous only reflections of the way we were brought up?

The key word is *only*. Good habits are a great Christian grace, and a lifetime of Christian works is something to be coveted and cultivated. But if our righteousnesses are only that—if there is no passion there, no commitment, no conscious connection with the One who has forgiven us and remade us, and who now seeks to use us to do his will on earth as it is done in heaven—that's pretty tedious stuff. After all, Jesus came into this world not just to die for us. He came to live in us. He died and rose again to forgive us—certainly he did—but also to empower us. That's a radical thing about the Christian gospel. The Spirit of God is the active agent in our everlasting redemption and in our daily walk.

One of the reasons even church professionals can fail openly in the simplest Christian virtues (such as honesty and patience and gentleness) is that even when they're practicing them they may have gotten them separated somehow from the source that powers them. "Why should I knock myself out for this person when he does what he does to me?" is not an alien argument among those who cash church paychecks, fill the elective offices, or offer caring ministry in the local congregation. Why, indeed! Knocking one's self out—serving—has nothing to do with what people do for us. It has to do with Christ. It has to do with what goes on in your heart, which, in turn, has everything to do with what went on at Calvary two thousand years ago.

Half the drudgery of church labor relates to the fact that

God is less real to us than he is to the person who actively denies him. St. Paul left us with this curious prescription for daily work: filled "with the knowledge of his will ... that you may live a life worthy of the Lord and may please Him in every way: bearing fruit in every good work" (Col. 1:9, 10). What's he talking about?

What flattens out ministry for many a church worker is the way we either resentfully refuse or willfully neglect to equate the day-to-day drudgery of life with the will of God— what God wants. We think we aren't bearing fruit for him in every little thing we do.

No wonder our ministries are not a joy any more. We plod through the same old daily routine with the same old worries plucking at our sleeves. We don't see that it's all part of God's thoughtful will, for us and for his church. No wonder we ask ourselves what difference we make and what good we are doing. We're not factoring God into our daily service. Without God—a real God—what you do is haphazard, random, and, at best, mildly positive. But when you take seriously your God and your work in his name, then what you do fits like a tile into the overall mosaic of God's purpose and his plan. Then what you do counts.

St. Paul, of course, had met God face-to-face. Out there in the desert, with his back to the dust of the Damascus road and his eyes blinded from the brilliance that was hovering over him, Paul had actually talked to God—or, rather, he had listened. That's the way you come to take God seriously. You talk to him and listen.

Many go through life never once talking to God, and then they complain he isn't real to them. But let a person begin each day with God to plot the next twenty-four hours in a joint planning session with the great I AM himself. Pause every now and then for an aside with the glorious One who said, "I am with you always." Step into his private chapel and pace the worn spot on the rug to debrief before the real overseer of your ministry. Close the books at night and turn them in for audit to the glorious bookkeeper of the heavenly enterprise, and then turn out the lights. God then becomes serious business. Talk to God!

And listen. That's the other half of our prayer life which desperately needs our attention. There are not many good listeners about, and even fewer who listen to the voice of God. Because of that, some of us equate our own words with "what he saith," or we wonder what God is trying to say, as if God were at a loss to make himself clear. But God communicates. He communicates well. He inspired the greatest book of all time in order to communicate with us. Of course you have to read it: the Bible. You have to shove your own preoccupations and opinions to the side, and quash down the noise of worry, distraction, anxiety, and the clamor for your own gratification, to hear his still, small voice. The echo of God's voice is not that distant. Talk to him. Listen to him. He's real.

Malcolm Muggeridge is reported to have said, "I have found the devil easier to believe in than God; for one thing, alas, I have had more to do with him." Sad, but he makes a point. You can't take God seriously if you have little or nothing to do with him.

For Group or Personal Reflection
1. Have you ever hated or denied God? Share any of those possible times. In retrospect, how close were you to God in Christ at those times?
2. Where is God right now in your life?
3. Assuming none of us is perfect, try to assess how much of your Christian life is habit and how much is pro-active faith?
4. What is the will of God for your life?
5. How much do you talk to God? How much do you listen to God? What might make it difficult to listen?

To Take This One Step Farther
1. Set aside five minutes in the morning and five minutes at night to talk to God. Actually verbalize your thoughts.

Don't allow yourself to run down or give out before your five minutes elapse. If you have no more to say, say it all over again or try the Lord's Prayer.

2. Set aside an additional five minutes each morning and each evening to listen. Just quiet everything down. Listen hard. Try to identify the "still, small voice." Note that he speaks by bringing Bible words and concepts to mind.

Prayer

> **Savior of my soul, you are so often closest to me when I feel farthest from you, and near at hand in those moments when I think you have forsaken me. Make your presence known to me and your reality a certainty. Let me hear your voice and feel your presence every passing hour. Then will I confess with all my heart that you are my God. Amen.**

Chapter 7

Right in the Middle of It All

*Who shall separate us from the love of Christ?
Shall trouble or hardship or persecution or
famine or nakedness or danger or sword? . . .
No, in all these things we are more than con-
querors through him who loved us.* Rom.
8:35, 37

Not many people remember Henry Drummond, and it isn't
terribly essential that they do so. It's more important to remember some of the things he said. He was a master at cap-
sulating truth, squeezing enormous notions and profound
concepts into little, quotable, adage-sized sentences. One of
the things that doesn't sound like much at first blush is "keep
in the middle of life." When you peel apart the layers of truth
and verity which produced it, you recognize not only the
truth of the matter but the genius of the man who thought
of it.

Recognize, first of all, that it is not the advice most of us
have been looking for. Some plan, some ambition of yours,
goes frightfully wrong and you feel like chucking the whole
thing, letting others try their hands at it. You attempt earnestly
to offer care to people in your congregation. However, you
get nothing but trouble for your trouble, and you wonder
why in heaven's name you should keep sticking your neck
out for others to chop at. Why expose yourself so that others
can beat you about the ears?

For example, one of the evangelism callers becomes ov-
erbearing with a prospect, and the whole calling program
comes into question, and all its participants become suspect.

Somebody on the church council does something which is not up to the Christian standard, and half the congregation blames the pastor for not doing something about it, as if he were the culprit who had "done wrong" in the first place.

So you say to yourself, "I didn't ask for this." All the while out there in the back of your mind is that nostalgic dream about being a hermit on a South Sea island somewhere, where life is all waving palm fronds and gazing out to sea. Here comes Drummond to tell you to stay right in the middle of it all. It reminds you of St. Peter and what he laid down in his first epistle, "If you suffer for doing good and you endure it, this is commendable before God" (1 Pet. 2:20). Commendable! It calls for a Distinguished Service Cross.

Why? Why should you stay in the middle? Why shouldn't you toss it all overboard? Over the years, one idea, as shocking as it sounds and as likely as it is to raise an argument, has helped almost as much as the gospel of grace to see me through. It is this: our purpose in life, yours and mine, is not, first of all, to be happy, at least not in the way we like to think about happiness.

As hard as that sounds, one of the great helpful insights for the church worker is the discovery that Christian ministry is not designed to make your life easy. It has other goals entirely. Gratifying as your life of service may be, it has this other side to it, the side which is intended to lay hold of ugly situations and make something out of them. That's the other half which we tend to forget, the creative half. It's the kingdom of God you're building. It costs something to build a kingdom: a bit of your pride, maybe, or some personal advancement or prosperity. It costs something. "Thy will be done," we pray. Well, that will is aiming at the redemption of human life, and redemption is expensive. Go to Calvary. Look around. You'll see. And then remember, "Hereunto are you called."

Recognize, in the second place, there's a lot to be gained by staying in the middle of things, not hiding or isolating yourself and abdicating your responsibilities. There is, for example—there in the middle—the chance to practice what you preach, to use your Christian gifts, to exercise your Christian virtues. There—in the middle—is the opportunity to flex the muscles of your faith and your commitments.

How do you get good at something? You practice. If people don't exercise their arms they develop no biceps at all. If a person does not exercise his soul and the virtues with which the Spirit of God endows that soul (Gal. 5:22, 23), he develops no strength of character, no moral vigor, no inner beauty, and above all, no ability to fall back on his Lord, no strength in his fingertips to hang on to Jesus when the bottom falls out.

What great, good fortune is yours as a pastor, teacher, DCE, volunteer, Stephen Minister, a worker in the church! You not only have the opportunity, you have the necessity to handle the Word of God and put it into daily practice. Nothing benefits a Christian more than that. We talk about the responsibilities of church work. They don't begin to compare with the privileges which attend working in God's vineyard, the privilege of daily opportunity to practice Christian virtues. Practice, you know, makes perfect.

We all know people who have opted out, telling us "much obliged" but they don't care for the kind of thing Jesus got himself into, if that's what church work entails, or the perils of city and sea that Paul kept walking into, or the jail where Peter spent the night. If honesty is to be cheated, kindness abused, gentleness trodden under foot, and truth nailed to a cross, why stay in it with nothing but God-talk to protect you?

I don't know why church work needs to be so hard. I don't have a full deck of easy explanations why things are as they are, to deal out a few every time something goes wrong. I certainly don't know the reasons for the difficulties you are facing at the moment. I do know that quitting—getting out of the middle—is not the answer. Jesus is. He's in it with you, with his body broken and blood spilled to make you strong.

Sometimes at the end of a long day when the muscles of body, mind, and spirit have begun to sag, it's easy to fall victim to the deep sigh, the feeling of dejection. That's a good time to remember it is in the middle of things, where everything is clamor and turmoil, there, right there, that a special blessing may be had. Not off in some corner protected from the cruel things that happen in this world, not in some safety zone. Drummond has it right: "Keep in the middle of life." That's where the crowns are handed out; that's where the benefits are being ladled up; that's where a person learns first hand what it means to walk with Jesus.

For Group or Personal Reflection

1. When was the last time you felt like "chucking it all"? What did you end up doing? What resources did you draw on?
2. Did you ever suffer for doing good? What happened?
3. Are there ever times when it might be helpful temporarily to get out of the middle of life, at least for awhile? What might those times be and what might you do temporarily?
4. When might you have been tempted to say "My will be done" rather than "Thy will be done"?
5. How in particular might you "exercise your soul"?

To Take This One Step Farther

1. Isolate the items on this day's agenda which make its prospects less than happy. Identify the Christian attitude or virtue which they call for. Now consider that rather than merely tackling the agenda item, you are practicing a Christian virtue in Christ's power. Your day will be a lot happier.
2. Reference Gal. 5:22–23. With which of these fruit of the Spirit does your Christian maturity need practice? Take one a day and practice.

Prayer

I ask not to be spared, O blessed Jesus; I plead no special privilege. Where you send me, I will go. What you commission to be done, I will do it. When you speak, like Samuel of old, I listen. Move me to respond in your service to what you in service have given me. Amen.

Chapter 8

Rights, Right, and Righteousness

Here is a trustworthy saying that deserves full acceptance: Christ Jesus came into the world to save sinners—of whom I am the worst. But for that very reason I was shown mercy so that in me, the worst of sinners, Christ Jesus might display his unlimited patience as an example for those who would believe on him and receive eternal life. 1 Tim. 1:15, 16

It's better to be right than sorry. But there's not a good deal more to be said for being right. I mean, it's not the top of the list of things for Christians to be, as if it were the ultimate in Christian attainment. It is certainly not carte blanche to do things that, standing alone, offend the standards set down by God for the behavior of his people.

Someone blatantly runs down the reputation and does damage to the good name of a sister or a brother. When you ask him how he can do that, he answers, "Well, it's true." Oh. That makes it right? It's not only in church where "right" is elevated way beyond its worth. Our world punishes error and esteems the revelation of truth, particularly lurid truth. "I'll let you in on the truth about him," we say, and lower our voices for emphasis. We have made a fetish out of the public's "right to know" the truth, particularly the damaging truth, no matter what the consequences of such open knowledge may be. Some celebrity commits an indiscretion, some public figure is involved in a divorce action, and suddenly we have not only the right but the duty to focus upon a detailed review of his or her life, starting with grade school and running right up to the minute. And just as suddenly, at this point, accuracy has the privilege to give way to best guess, and precision yields to surmise.

I don't know where the right to know came from, or who conveyed upon me the privilege to sift through anybody's dirty laundry. I do know it does not make for good (in the best sense of that word) reading or listening, no matter how many copies of it sell at the supermarket checkout stand.

But let's not move away from the point. Right, accuracy, and genuineness do not lead the parade of Christian preoccupations. Don't get me wrong. Right has its place. Right is important and right is right. But it isn't everything. There are better things to be than right. It is really shocking when right is overly extolled in the church. People who strive mightily for exoneration, vindication, or to win the day for their particular points of view—as if those were of first-rate importance—neglect the central truth of Christianity. Christ came into the world to forgive sins. He is champion not of the right but of the repentant, and is not much impressed by human rightness.

Of course, we doff our hats to the importance of preserving without error the doctrinal positions which were so hard won on the historic battlefields of church history. May I be forgiven for this outrage upon our sensitivities, but even here, being right must be servant to being effective conveyers of the gospel of peace. And it can be.

Being right is not an end in itself. Once you've been given the truth—and that's what it is, a gift not an accomplishment—the question is, what are you going to do with it? How shall it serve your real purpose in life—to offer hope to sinners, to model victory for the lost, and to rally for the benefit of those not yet in Christ the efforts of the churches we serve?

I'm all for being right and standing on the side of rightness and goodness and justice. But being right, in the sense that we've got the picture when someone else does not, is not the end and goal of Christianity. On the scale of values which pertain for Christians, on the list of Christian priorities, being right is not rated half so highly as being forgiving and forgiven and open and winsome and attentive to everybody's point of view. Being right is a tool for being effective and faithful.

Some years ago when Christianity was not so exclusively verbal, it included a lot more effort to do something about it. Many Christian homes practiced the custom of giving up something for Lent, a reminder that Calvary took precedence over the pleasures of life. I'm by nature a little chary of piety which is overly apparent. But I wish we might forgo, especially during Lent, all our preoccupation with how right we are.

Nothing seems to me more inappropriate than emphasizing that we are right during that season of the church year when the Christian story and its hero, Jesus, concentrate on all the "poor little devils" who can't get anything right. When Jesus made that awful walk all the way to the top of the hill, he wasn't concerned with the righteous (except inasmuch as our righteousnesses are like filthy rags) but with those who find themselves helpless to be right.

Of course, I have an advantage at this point. I'm not right often enough to find much comfort in it. But even such as are inevitably right might be well advised to consider their rightness a gift of God's grace, thank him for it, and quit swinging it around like a cudgel as if there were some special credit accruing. The message of the Christian religion is inappropriate unless we get our focus off our rightness and zero in on humanity's desperate need for One to be right for us, for the Son of God to die for us, not because we are so right but because we are so terrifyingly wrong.

Just in case you think we're going around with no purpose at all, consider what happens just at the level of your own heart. What is the focus of your comfort there? When someone questions you—your integrity, your judgment—to what do you automatically appeal? Isn't it usually the fact that in your mind and heart you are right?

St. Paul began every exercise of self-assessment with a confession. One was so abject you think at first it is just in a manner of speaking. "Sinners, of whom I am the worst ... " (1 Tim. 1:15). But he really meant it. He observed from the bottom of the pile the panorama of Christian truth and saw at the top of it not the importance of rightness. He saw the preeminence of God's love in Christ.

Start with this, "I am in all respects wrong. But Jesus loves me thus and died for me and made me right again. When I open my mouth, I will reflect—I will focus upon, I will raise to the top—God's grace for me and for all."

For Group or Personal Reflection

1. When might you have been "right" about something or someone and later you realized that it didn't really matter?
2. When has it been most difficult for you to forgive?
3. What are examples of times that being right must be servant to being effective conveyors of the gospel of peace?
4. What are some truths you have been given that you can use to serve others?
5. If we forgo a preoccupation with how right we are, what can this do for us personally? When we do this, what can it do for others?

To Take This One Step Farther

Identify one person who needs your love this day. How will you open your hands and heart to that person?

Prayer

Another day of grace and love! How can I thank you, Lord? For a deceitful heart and haughty thoughts, for barbed words honed on secret pride, for thoughtlessness and un-called-for boldness, for improper vanity— Lord, pity me. For every failure to model your mercy and your gentleness so freely shared, forgive me. For every missed opportunity to display your total compassion and forbearance, grant pardon. And for ev-

ery hint that my greatest claim is superiority—for such pride and poor priority, forgive me and be patient. Give me grace to reorder my life to highlight your kind of love and concern for those with whom I interact. Keep me ever mindful that anything of which I may properly boast is a free, unmerited gift from you. Amen.

Chapter 9

The Parable of the Selenium

Come near to God and he will come near to you. James 4:8

For me to employ scientific phenomena for purposes of illustration puts the entire process into jeopardy, inasmuch as I have no solid base of scientific knowledge in which to root this. Having negotiated the better part of an entire lifetime in this world with reasonably good fortune, for which I am properly grateful to my God, I have nonetheless done so (remarkably enough when you consider the focus of our recent history) maintaining only a nodding acquaintance with the great scientific conclusions of our day. For me the hard and cold facts of scientific discovery are pretty much in the realm of hearsay. Nevertheless, in what follows, the facts have been checked and are reliable, although scientific jargon is avoided.

There is an element commonly found as a byproduct of copper mining, which has a startling property as regards the conducting of electricity, When it is itself in bright light, it serves as an excellent conductor of electricity; in fact, it can turn light directly into electricity. But the dimmer the light which surrounds it, the more sluggish the flow of electricity through it, until at last, when it is in total darkness, it actually acts as a resistor, hindering electric current. This phenomenon provides such an ideal parable I can't pass up the chance to remark about it.

It doesn't require great mental effort to appreciate how appropriate an illustration this scientific principle is when addressing the unique subcategory of humans we've been calling church workers. Anyone who has worked a week and

a half in denominational administration or within the struc-
ture of a local congregation—or is a responsible leader of a
faculty in a church related school or service institution—
knows that church workers fall into one of two categories.
They are conductors or they are resistors.

The conductors are those through whom enthusiasm, programs, ideas, insights, and even the revelation of God through
the holy Word, flow like the Amazon River from the high
country of their source to the fertile bottom lands where the
people live, move, and have their being.

There are, however, disastrously, resistors in the ranks
too. Frustrated administration types call these "bottlenecks,"
among other things. These are the enablers who refuse to let
a program be enabled. These are the church workers at whose
doorstep innovative ideas come to rest—everlasting rest.
These are the ones who field whatever enthusiasm has been
generated, as surely as Ozzie Smith, and nail it before it gets
to first base. We have plenty around us, and, sometimes,
within us, which presumes it has done its Christian duty by
throwing cold water on every "new-fangled" program which
comes along, or by sparing the members of the congregation
the necessity of making a decision by shielding them from
certain information or options.

The properties of selenium suggest at this point that what
makes church workers resistors or conductors has to do with
their relation to the light. To be sure, there may be legitimate
reasons for not passing along some denominationally-begot
program to the local family of the faithful. But for now, go
along for the sake of the point. The Light, the great Light, the
Light of the world, is Jesus himself. When a person stands in
that Light, and when that Light shines on him, he becomes,
generally, an efficient conductor of the love of Christ, of enthusiasm for the kingdom of God and its commerce, and of
zeal for those efforts and programs which seek to make the
kingdom come. Like a selenium photoelectric cell, he turns
Christ's light into electricity for the good of others.

The opposite is at least as true: the farther one stands from the Light of life, the more resistance he provides to its flow. Sometimes a person is out in the dark altogether, and the current of energy from Christ and Christ-like things does not flow through him to others at all.

St. John likes to utilize the most startling contrasts to explain the difference that Christ makes. Jesus spells life, he says. Without Jesus is death (John 1:4). Startling difference! Jesus is light. Not knowing Jesus causes people to wander aimlessly in total darkness (John 12:35).

His point is the totality, the "utterly," of the difference that Christ makes. But might we not, for our purposes, properly focus on the degrees of difference that Jesus makes? The closer your walk with him, the more efficient the flow from Christ through you to the Christians whom you serve. Not only to Christians, either.

The parable pertains most effectively at the point where church workers funnel to the non-Christian world. Church workers sometimes go to great lengths to convince the world that they and those they represent are quite different. But to facilitate the flow from the cross to the unbeliever (and what's the point if that isn't it?), the process requires, depends upon, and relates specifically to the closeness of the conductor to the Light, who is Jesus. He makes the great difference.

You won't need a blow to the head or the heart to get the point. What you and I need, and all workers in the church need, is a block of extra time each day to mull that over. The pointed lesson the parable of the selenium makes—the specific suggestions for our lives which spring from it—will occur to us when we get down, brother, when we get down, sister, and ponder this: my service to church and world flows and ebbs in direct relationship to my closeness to or distance from the Light of Jesus.

Oh yes, to polish off the picture: when all of us standing square under the Light of the world become super-efficient conductors of God's Word, ways, and will, then our lives, our parishes, our denominations, and all Christendom will light up and stand out against the sky like a city set on a hill. That is what God has in mind.

For Group or Personal Reflection

1. In what ways are you a conductor? In what ways are you a resistor?
2. How can you stand in the Light and become more of a conductor and less of a resistor? Be specific.
3. How can you equip others to stand in the Light so they can become conductors?
4. How do you turn the Light into electricity for the benefit of others? How are you a "little Christ," as Luther says?
5. Read Eph. 4:7–16. What does the Light have to do with what is described there?

To Take This One Step Farther

1. Set apart one week for a special focused pattern of personal devotional activity. Intensify your attention to the words of the Bible as you ponder during your devotions. Then monitor the qualitative difference which a more intense and focused walk with Jesus makes.
2. Ponder this: What are some denominational resources that could benefit your congregation, which you as a caregiver can use to become a conductor, rather than a resistor?

Prayer

I want always to stand in the brightness of your truth and the sunshine of your smile, dear Lord. Move me toward an ever closer walk with you. Give me greater patience in my hope and more constancy in my Christian love, for your name's sake. Amen.

Chapter 10

Your Symbol Quotient

*In everything set them an example by doing
what is good. In your teaching show integrity, seriousness and soundness of speech that
cannot be condemned, so that those who op-
pose you may be ashamed because they have
nothing bad to say about us.* Titus 2:7–8

Reggie Jackson is not just a former major league baseball
player. He is a symbol for prolific bat production in the late
season, particularly in World Series play. They called him "Mr.
October." Jerry West was not simply a great basketball player.
He was a symbol for coming through when the chips are
down. Chick Hearn called him "Mr. Clutch." Willie Mays was
not just a center fielder. He was a symbol for power hitting
and errorless fielding. They used to tag him "Old Faithful."
Bobby Fisher—just a chess player? Oh, no! He was the symbol
of an irascible personality. "Don't pull a Bobby Fisher" meant
you shouldn't be easily provoked. You should have a longer
fuse.

Let's talk about your symbol quotient. On the plane the
burly fellow in 19 C turns to you and asks, "What business
are you in?" His errant grammar notwithstanding, you reply,
"I work in the church." He needs elaboration. "What do you
do?" He wants to know the essence of your position, your
station in life. He's after your job description. He's made a
mistake. His question is valid, but only later, down the line a
ways.

Your efficacy as a church worker does not consist in the
first place in what you do. It isn't to be discovered—not at
its best and highest—by a review of the accompanying letter

that came with your call, or the documents which fix the parameters of your responsibilities. Your leadership is not—in its initial instance or most significant aspect—what you do. It is rooted in the God who called you, the Lord whose servant you are, and it is expressed by *how* you are. Your leadership is expressed in the first place by an aura you bring with you when you walk into a room.

Adolf Hitler is a symbol. So is Ben Franklin, George Wallace, and Martin Luther King—and Harry Kleinschmidt. Harry Kleinschmidt? Sure. He's the janitor in one of our local congregations. His pastor says that at the office when Harry comes in, everybody brightens up. That's the kind of church worker he is. His symbol quotient is "pleasant." It's not what he does; it's *how* he is. He stands for something, something good.

What do people think when they see you? How do people feel when you come on the scene? Here's a related question which helps us measure our symbol quotient: Whom do people go to when they need something? We can all tell the time-honored stories about fabled heroes in the church—the homiletics prof whose socks never matched or the big wig in the regional office who could not be counted upon to get to the right terminal at LAX or the Kennedy or Dallas Airports, or who forever "lost" his glasses after pushing them back on the top of his head. There are other distinctions too: the Sunday School teachers who were tough, pastors who were especially caring, volunteers who never said no. Here are some symbols from which we might well demur:

a. Thoughtlessness—being overly concerned for our points of view or about the rigors of our ministries; failing to put ourselves in other people's shoes; tactlessness

b. Stuffiness—leaving the impression behind us that we rate ourselves pretty highly, and consider our accomplishments quite remarkable and our intelligence unique

c. Negativism—putting down the earnest attempts of other folks to be productive and to do productive things; seeing and surfacing the weaknesses and imperfections of every and all except #1

d. Quarrelsomeness—lining up the anti ducks; depleting the enthusiasm and siphoning off the support of all

e. Jealousy—impugning motives; being suspicious and demanding

Here are some symbols to which you might aspire:

a. Positivism—raising up the best in everything; seeing and serving the possibilities

b. Enthusiasm—warmth, interest and ardor

c. Happiness—joy, contentment, cheer, satisfaction

d. Putting the best construction on everything (I'm convinced one week of this on the part of all the workers of the church would so drastically alter the direction of Christendom that our Lord's fondest dreams and Christianity's most earnest hopes would move within instant reach.)

e. Calm reaction and measured spirit—this is the aura which verifies our trust that all is ever in God's hands, that nothing permanently damaging can happen to God's people, that never, ever, is there a need for language that goes to extremes or for actions which panic the peace of God's people.

For a more complete listing of appropriate symbol goals for church workers, read Gal. 5:22–23 (over and over again).

The element common to the two lists above, conspicuous in the second by its absence, is YOU. Take yourself out of the descriptions and list one gives way to list two. Martin Luther favored daily drowning for what he called (with scriptural support) the "old Adam," the "old self" (Romans 6:6). That may seem at first blush to be severe, but a second thought reminds us that the alternative to self at the center of life is Christ, and Christ at the center of life alters for the better in drastic ways the quality of our quotient symbols.

I have been present when responsible people have contemplated the church and its failures, wrung their hands and asked, "What shall we do?" I'm always tempted to answer, "Nothing." The answer isn't forever in doing something. The answer more often than not is *being* something. Be a good symbol. Be a symbol of those quotients which mark the children of God and leaders of his kingdom. The process is simple. With Christ's cross, cross out your old self and let Jesus stand in its stead. Believe me, you'll stand for something and Someone then.

For Group or Personal Reflection
1. Who are you? *How* are you?
2. What is your symbol quotient?
3. What symbol or symbols might characterize you that you would rather be rid of?
4. What symbol or symbols do you not currently possess that you aspire to?
5. What constitutes effective leadership?

To Take This One Step Farther
1. After choosing one Christian virtue that you aspire to, post it somewhere near your work place as a reminder of the aura for which you are striving in the Spirit.
2. Spend a brief moment every morning in earnest prayer that Jesus may help you be the kind of church worker who exudes that virtue.

Prayer

> O divine Love, who can make even me to be what you desire, when others look at me, your child, let them see one who is just and true and good; one who puts right before gain, and others before self; things of the Spirit before things of this world; principles before reputation; and you before all else. Amen.

Chapter 11

This Is a Personal Matter

If we claim to be without sin, we deceive our-
selves and the truth is not in us. If we confess
our sins, he is faithful and just and will for-
give us our sins and purify us from all un-
righteousness. 1 John 1:8–9

There are two styles by which some acknowledge their sins, which are, for the most part, ineffective, and which in fact militate against the essence of confession. (I mean the confession of our sins.) One way to take the sting out of confession and pull its teeth (to mix the metaphor and addle the comparison) is to confess to sin in general. "I am, I readily admit, less honest than I ought to be," or, "I would hate to tally all the wicked notions which pass across the monitor of my mind in a given week"; even "chief of sinners though I be."

The problem with such broad-stroke admission of guilt is its lack of focus. It diffuses the effectiveness of confession. We confess our sins in general and thereby don't feel the need to confess any in particular. To take upon yourself the general guiltiness of mankind can be just another way of diluting any personal guilt of your own.

Church workers are masters at this. Perhaps that is because church workers do a lot of confessing in public. Easy admissions to inherent wickedness roll off the tongue with some facility when you're teaching a Bible class or conducting a youth rally. That's one reason the Scriptures commend a closet as an appropriate locale for prayer and confession (Matt. 6:6 KJV). There is not much room in a closet for an audience. No audience will translate into no advantage in watering down confession with generalities. In a closet one tends to become very specific. Knowing what you know about yourself, it's hard to fool yourself with vagueness. Go off somewhere all by yourself. Then try counting your transgressions; name them one by one. Don't lose yourself in the panorama of the world's imperfection.

A second device by which the confession of sins has been disarmed and neutered is the slick art of confessing the sins of other people. Most everybody these days is so busy confessing the sins of others that they don't harbor a great deal of concern for their own. Interestingly, that, too, pertains particularly in the church—and with a vengeance. How long has it been since you heard someone at church say, "It seems I was wrong," or, "I wish now I hadn't said that," or, "I'm sorry"? More important, how long has it been since you have said something like that?

Twice now in the past week, speakers have referred in my hearing to that familiar question in the account which documents the institution of the Holy Sacrament, "Is it I?" This is not a question you hear often in our day. If the disciples had been minded that night in the upper room to ask our kind of questions, it would have come out, "Is it old Peter again, Lord?" or, "Did you ever consider the problems posed by the unseemly ambitions of James and John and above all their mother?" or "I may be no paragon of sainthood, but there are several around this table whose particular sins I would like respectfully to confess."

Our church life, our responsibilities in the church and out of it, our spiritual being—these are an intensely personal affair and revolve around specifics. This is true of all of Christianity. The Father and the Son through the Spirit call you by your name. At the end of the day you stand before the great HIMSELF alone, and when the alarm tugs you out of sleep in the morning, it's just you and his orders of the day. Through it all God cares for you minute by minute and very specifically.

I recall the ramifications of Hab. 2:4 as I learned it as a boy in catechetical class. "The righteous shall live by his faith."

But we were taught, when we recited that gem, to make "his" jump right off the page. "The righteous shall live by *his* faith," not the faith of anyone else—mother, aunt or grandad. It's everyone for himself at this point. We're on our own before God. "Just as I am." Except, of course, that Jesus stands with you, walks with you, and gives his angels charge over you. But the trust, the confidence, the hand in the hand of Jesus— all free gifts from a gracious God—must nonetheless be yours, your very own.

The sins are ours, too. The road around and through our failures and our wickedness is a road each of us must walk. The question is not "What's with them?" but, "Is it I?" That road, with your feet on it, wends its way to the top of Golgotha, to the cross and forgiveness and renewal and another chance. It's all freely given and arranged and directed by God, and involves the hearts and hands of his people.

That opens the door to let in an additional thought on the subject, and then we can leave it go at that. There is another way to diffuse and nearly nullify confession. A recent spectacle on a very public scale in connection with the collapse and disgrace of some of the large electronic ministries in our nation (though it's not uncommon on the local scene, and that's why I surface it at all) has shown us confessors who seek to orchestrate their own forgiveness and rehabilitation.

With his confession, sometimes quite specific, even before the ink has dried, so to speak, the confessor is giving specific instructions to assure that as God forgives, so will the Board of Elders, and as God uses remade and renewed sinners, so must "my denomination or my congregation, and I want to make that amply clear." If generalities, if pointing to the failures of others, diffuses and destroys the effectiveness of confession, then assuming the role of maestro for the symphony that plays the sweet music of absolution and rehabilitation does as well.

"Is it I, Lord?" is an appropriate way to end the day, and to begin it too. Then let the glorious gospel go into gear. Keep your hands off. Put yourself in everlasting arms. It all works better that way.

For Group or Personal Reflection

1. How do you confess your sins?
2. What struggles have you had in confessing your sins?
3. (Answer this question only if you feel comfortable doing so.) What is one sin you need to confess which, as yet, you have not?
4. Which biblical character are you most like in your sinfulness?
5. How can Christ help you ask the penetrating and exposing question "Is it I?"?

To Take This One Step Farther

1. Check the list that follows and flag those words that call to mind some experience of failure, some weakness, even some intentional sin on your part: insolence, hatred, strife, jealousy, anger, factiousness, dissension. (If this list has a familiar ring, note it is a simple rewrite of Gal. 5:19–21.)
2. Spend the next few moments in solitude to confess specific sins—yours. Name them one by one. Ask for and be assured of forgiveness in Christ.

Prayer

> **Set me free, my Lord, from self-will and rebellion in my heart, from discontent with my lot and unwillingness to do my duty. Lead me on that path which leads to fulfillment of your purposes. May my love for my fellow humans grow deeper, and my devotion to you and your kingdom more profound. Amen.**

Chapter 12

Making the Most of Them

*The man who plants and the man who waters
have one purpose, and each will be rewarded
according to his own labor. For we are God's
fellow workers.* 1 Cor. 3:8–9

Some of the eyes which scan this page belong to such as could be termed "church staff." They labor for and in the church, and they do that "in the braces" with other church workers. In most instances church workers are part of a team. And therein lies the makings of a problem. To be part of a team, to be staff, raises its own set of challenges.

Not all of those challenges and not every staff-related problem settles down upon the shoulders of the lower echelon. Being #1 is not always an English walk-about either. To be responsible for the work of others, and to carry on a ministry that is partly dependent and certainly judged by the quality of the labor of others, leaves a person vulnerable and a little sensitive too.

Usually the special burdens which accompany team effort are felt most heavily by the people on the nether end of the pecking order. "Those who direct our work don't understand. Their labor, their judgment, their instincts and their philosophies are themselves inferior. If only we were free to do it our way, we could accomplish so much more." Or, "I do all the work and he gets all the credit." Second fiddle, for a whole catalogue of reasons, is a very difficult instrument to play and even harder to master.

Church workers are not automatically apt when it comes to working as part of a staff. That's sad, since it is to every worker's advantage to make the most of his coworkers and the work that they do. What CEOs suspect is true. Their effectiveness rating is dependent upon the quality of the work their staff and volunteer workers put out.

But that's just as true for all of us who work in the church, no matter what our position is. One staffer falls on his face, and everyone looks like a dummy. Egg ends up on the face of more than just the volunteer whose spoon misses his mouth. Sometimes the failure of one worker contributes to the downfall of another, as when the church secretary announces in the parish paper an erroneous and totally spurious starting time for the walk-a-thon in support of world relief. (Where did that come from? Is my staff out to torpedo my boat?) At other times it's just the general perception that the entire staff is mediocre because of the ineptness of one.

Doesn't this suggest some value for staff people to consciously support, assist, improve, and approve the efforts and labors of their fellows? Here are some suggestions for making the most of your compatriot servants in the church:

a. Never, ever, even under the most extreme circumstances, speak ill of a fellow worker. If a negative assessment is required, tell only the villain himself and in a way that helps. (Leering and snorting are, as a rule, not productive.)

The Navy has a helpful arrangement. It has created the rank of the petty officer. It's his assignment to focus on the small stuff, thus freeing everyone else for more productive tasks. The church has no comparable arrangement, though the idea has some merit. Too many assume for themselves the responsibilities of pettiness. At any rate, there are plenty of others around to fill the vacuum created when you abstain from such critical activity.

b. Put the best construction on what your fellow workers do or say. I have spent a great deal of time around church workers, and I have never known one who wasn't trying to work to the glory of God and the good of God's people. Not everything they do necessarily accomplishes those purposes, but their intentions are good. I'd wager on that. Every one of them was in dead earnest about the Christian faith and its priority in the life of people. That's a plus, and we might do well to keep it in mind.

Not one of them, secondly, was perfect. Think of the problem you would have if even one of the people on your staff was 100% perfect. That would be grounds for your instant resignation, believe me. Nor was even one of them so poor the Holy Spirit couldn't use him, if there were enough prayers from his fellow staffers asking for that.

And, finally, I never met one who did not respond better to the loving word of support as opposed to carping criticism. Many of us have criticism coming, no question about it, but just by way of being practical, the kind word produces a great deal more than a sharp one does.

Somewhere between 40% and 80% (you figure it in your case) of our negative feelings about a staff member have nothing to do with him anyway. A great deal of the contrariness we feel about others is just a defensive reaction to the deep disappointment we feel in ourselves for the poor caliber of work we've been turning in of late, or the poor judgment we have exercised, or the goldbricking of which we have been guilty. We are programmed to attribute our failures to the fault of other people, to hide our second-rate contributions behind a smokescreen of disapproval and criticism of the other fellow's work.

There is at our disposal a most effective style for dealing with our personal frustrations and self-blame which doesn't involve those with whom we work at all, at least not as our scapegoats. It's called the cross, and it features a Savior. Jesus, so this comfort reminds us, judges us on faithfulness, not production. He asks how earnestly you have tried, not how totally you have succeeded. He seems to lose interest after he has gauged your effort and goes on to other things once he perceives that the endeavor was zealously attempted.

He treats the others on your team the same way. It's one team, one ministry, with varying responsibilities for each. We aren't stuck with each other; we are joined to each other, and the glue that binds us and makes us one is Christ, and our commitment to him, or better yet, his to us. And that, in turn, is the source and the strength of our commitment to each other.

For Group or Personal Reflection

1. What are the benefits and costs of being the team leader?
2. What are the benefits and costs of being other than the leader of the team?
3. In what areas might you have weaknesses as a team player?
4. In what areas do you think you have strengths as a team member?
5. How can you become a better team player?

To Take This One Step Farther

1. Make a list of all the church workers with whom you are joined (e.g., fellow staff, other volunteers, etc.). Entitle it "team." Add them to your daily prayer list.
2. Select one fellow worker to whom on one day of the week you will say at least one supportive thing. (If you're really brave, try this sentence with him or her: "Is there anything that I can do, any way that I can help you?")

Prayer

Holy God, I would remember before your throne of grace all with whom I labor for your name's sake and all in the world who labor in the interests of your kingdom. Keep us from pride and envy. Control all we do, that it may be in accordance with your will. For my sake, Lord, and for yours, make effective the work of _____ and _____ , and

help me to see only one ministry here in this place, with each of us responsible for his part, and all of us responsible toward each other. Amen.

Chapter 13

It Does No Harm to Smile

With joy you will draw water from the wells of salvation. In that day you will say: "Give thanks to the Lord, call on his name; make known among the nations what he has done, and proclaim that his name is exalted. Sing to the Lord, for he has done glorious things; let this be known to all the world. Shout aloud and sing for joy, people of Zion, for great is the Holy One of Israel among you."
Isaiah 12:3–6

In the writings of Martin Luther you will find a passage which suggests that true joy cannot be bottled up in the heart without causing some outward evidence of it. "God is not offended by gaiety. A quiet heart which truly believes that God has been reconciled to me because of Jesus Christ . . . will result in a cheerful countenance and happy eyes" (Luther's Works, Vol. 12, p. 81).

I'm glad Martin Luther said that. It affirms a suspicion I have entertained over the years that cheer and goodwill and a happy face are appropriate tools for the church worker. The twelve elders of the congregation I served many years ago conspired with me to experiment with smiles. We made a contract with each other that over a twelve-week period each of us would try not to be caught without a smile for a whole meeting, during an entire worship service, for all of Sunday morning, or even during a chance encounter at the shopping center. We even set up a Rotary Club-type system of fines for failure to punctuate the process.

It all seemed a little childish at first, but it had some unexpected results. People in the congregation noticed. Initially they thought the elders knew something they didn't. Then they began to elbow each other as if they knew something the elders didn't. Pretty soon they began to smile. Smiling is a lot like German measles. Once it starts, it spreads. It's more contagious than rubella. Were you to try this, your whole congregation of saints could end up grinning and chuckling and generally beaming with glee and good will.

Luther, however, was not of a mind to put the cart before the horse. He would not suggest that smiles beget a happy and ecstatic heart. His point maintains the process in reverse. An ecstatic heart results in "happy eyes." It's inevitable. St. Paul wasn't fooling, and neither was the Holy Spirit who inspired him, when he insisted that the kingdom of God and membership in it isn't ho-hum "eating and drinking." It's "joy in the Holy Spirit" (Rom. 14:17).

Once Jesus makes a home in your heart, the result is "happy eyes" and the joy of your salvation. Wonderful things have happened to us because of the love of Christ. Those wonderful things make a person "glad in the Lord." Granted, there are moments (and doubtless more of them are related to the activities in the church than elsewhere) when silly grins are inappropriate. But look to the eyes. You can't mask the joy of your salvation behind your eyelids. If you've got it—a real grasp of what God's love means to you—it breaks out somewhere, and most apparently at that place where the windows open directly on the soul—your eyes.

The point could perhaps be made that too many who represent the church frequently produce an atmosphere quite lacking in glee. We spend an inordinate amount of our time reproving the erring, which requires a frown, or manifesting piety, which means you have to clench your teeth. Some live with the notion that seriousness and solemnity are synonyms. Somehow, between the heart and the lip, we let something slip. Where is the smile that corroborates the message of your ministry? If you believe what you preach, lecture about, teach, or share—what you presume to represent—it's going to squeak out somewhere in what passes for happiness.

When my German grandfather arrived in this country, he came under the burden of a middle name only the old country would think to employ: "Hilarious." Some of it has rubbed off. I have not taught a Bible class or preached a sermon when I did not feel it. It sets in after about five minutes and starts at the ankles and works its way up—an enthusiasm, even a glee, that bubbles and bounces and breaks out in mirth sooner or later. Funerals have been a problem at times. Restraint is appropriate given that setting, but restraint and the realization of God's grace in Jesus are not always easy companions. If you give way to the tendency of a "cheerful countenance" and "happy eyes"—particularly if you're my kind, which is apt to be overtaken totally by the merriment God's mercy creates—you may fall victim to the unguarded phrase or the undignified hop, skip, and leap.

There are New Testament stories which have the disciples expressing embarrassment over too manifest and enthusiastic a response to Christ and his ministering. But now and again a resounding "So what?" is in order. More people are attracted than repelled by the happy Christian. The opposite is certainly and particularly true: more people are repelled than are attracted by the sober, dignified, stuffy, flat-eyed, self-important representative of the Christian church.

So smile. Let a smile be your hallmark. Strange and wonderful things begin to happen to the one who smiles.

I have a pretty firm grip on the doctrine of the means of grace. God is the author of the fruits of faith, which, according to St. Paul (Gal. 5:22–23), are the marks of the Christian life. The means of grace are God's method for producing those fruit in our lives. I'm not suggesting that kind of stature for the common, everyday grin.

Nonetheless, I do believe that smiles alter the perspective in very helpful ways and hold open the heart to many of the by-products which attend the earnest believer, such as joy and peace and hope and certainty. (That may be too strong a statement. Opening the heart and holding it open are the Spirit's prerogative, and he's got his chosen tools for the job. But a smile does its best, at the very least, to keep us from clogging up the entrance and getting in the way.) The Bible may not recommend the out-and-out guffaw (Prov. 14:13; James 4:9), but it does risk a recommendation for a merry heart (Prov. 17:22).

For Group or Personal Reflection

1. What gets in the way of your smiling?
2. What causes you to smile?
3. Are there times you could or even should smile when currently you don't?
4. How might your smiling affect others? How might smiling affect you?
5. When is it inappropriate to smile?

To Take This One Step Farther

1. Thank God for three things that make you happy.
2. Tell a friend, a coworker, a stranger (that's best) three things that make you happy.
3. Stand in front of a mirror and observe as you state aloud three things that make you happy. Do it again. Look at yourself.

Prayer

Lift up my heart, dear God, and fill me with the joy of your salvation. Let me bring light and life and happiness to all with whom I have to do. Renew my spirit, and through me lift the spirits of all around me. Help me rejoice. Help me be glad. Help me sing praises to your holy name. Amen.

Chapter 14

All in Favor Please Say Aye

This is a trustworthy saying. And I want you to stress these things, so that those who have trusted in God may be careful to devote themselves to doing what is good. These things are excellent and profitable for everyone. Titus 3:8

All in favor please say aye. At the very least that would be refreshing. Commentaries on life in the ebbtide of the twentieth century rue the fact that negativism is so vocal. What is a greater regret and a more serious problem is the habitual silence of those who are for the most part "in favor." Contentment and agreeableness are under no compunction to express themselves, it would seem. As a result, the supportive get very little ink. They fade into the background and become so much a part of the scenery that they are invisible to the naked eye and inaudible in the cacophony of life.

For Christianity, the upshot is disastrous. At the heart of Christian faith is confession. It is in its essence partly proclamation. The substance of the Christian life is not what it is against. It is a vote and a voice in spirited favor of and devotion to Christ Jesus, God's Son, humanity's Savior and the "Lamb upon the throne." To sit back and bask wordlessly, without song or affirmation, in Christian conviction; or worse yet, to let negatives define the faith, telling all what Christians don't and aren't, misses the point and actually denies the essence of our religion.

Christianity is comprised of people who embrace the Christ and what he teaches. A person can, and many do, reject

77

cruelty and prejudice and dishonesty and all that the ancients tagged "iniquity," and be no Christian for all of that. To be Christian is to live and move and have one's being on the sunny, positive side of Christ's truth. It is being for, believing in and following after the One whom God has sent, his Son, who lived and died and rose and reigns for us forever. You can't fulfill your Christian destiny in the language of minuses and nots and denials.

Theologians at the time of the Reformation found it useful, after stating their convictions, to add what specific point they also rejected. Now and then the stress would lean toward what they did not believe. To define what one is against may be helpful, but not in itself. It is helpful only in the service of what *is* believed and esteemed.

The church you serve is at its heart not a negative, but a positive force. Its makeup consists of what it favors. The world around us and the brothers and sisters among us have the right to meet and know all those in favor. The ramifications are personal for church workers. Questions such as "How much of my day has been an expression of what the church favors?" or "How many of my words in the last twenty-four hours have expressed the positive truths we call 'the Christian faith'?" are an appropriate self-examination every now and again. We might be surprised and appalled at how much of our behavior and how many of our declarations define what we dislike and disown, as opposed to what great verities we approve.

That brings us to the second phrase in our title, which deserves triple bold: "Please say aye." This is an appeal of sorts, an earnest appeal, addressed to church workers to express their positive feelings. The agendas of the church in this day are not being set by mainstream, majority, positive people, nor is the present being toted into the future on their shoulders. Minority segments—often extreme in their perception of what is and ought to be, and very often negative—are imposing their focus and their will with frequency upon the church.

However, it is unfair to become upset with those few. They are, after all, filling a vacuum, which is a perfectly natural thing to do. And the point has nothing to do with the suggestion they are a minority. The point we're struggling to get to is that one whole, happy, diligent, contributing part of the total—be it small, medium or large—is not having its say in establishing points of focus and attention in the church, for no other reason than this odd penchant for being mute.

Please say aye. We need to hear that encouraging word. The church needs to hear that encouraging word. The Word is an encouraging word.

Let us concede, though it docs not come easily for me, that now and then a negative word is required. Would it not be a worthwhile experiment to investigate by trial whether you, your congregation, your church body, and the whole Christian church on earth would survive a three-week span during which only aye-sayers were vocal? Is this too protracted a period of time for the gainsayers to hold off? Why not institute a three-week span, in whatever realm you exercise some influence, during which all those who say they are in favor energetically say aye, and all those who are not give themselves the luxury of a deep breath and profound silence? Nothing would be lost in such a test, and some insight, some discovery, some serendipitous revelation might be gained.

After all, Christianity lives to proclaim the Good News, and those who are Christ's are committed to overcome their muteness and share with everyone the best news there is— that God in Christ is love, and in Christ God loves us all. It would seem that to sink into comfortable silence is not really an option for brothers and sisters in Christ.

What is it that determines your position in things churchly? Is it perhaps what you are against? Or is it what you are for, what you endorse, what you favor? If it is that, then for heaven's sake—for the sake of God and the church— please say that and promote that . . . and let the other go.

For Group or Personal Reflection
1. When do you feel most negative?
2. When do you feel most positive?
3. Are you ever too negative? When?
4. Are you ever too positive? When?
5. What practical things can you personally do to raise the "positivism level" of your congregation or area of ministry?

To Take This One Step Farther
1. Pause to contemplate what positive thought or theme for the church has failed to occupy its proper status in the daily agenda of the church. Determine to express your support for it at every opportunity for a full month. And then next month, do it again.
2. Consciously withdraw yourself, for a time at least, from those causes, those emphases, which are only against things.

Prayer

> **May the words of my mouth and the meditation of my heart be unfailing in support of your church and its cause. Deliver me from silence, and my tongue will sing of your righteousness. Amen.**

Chapter 15

To Reach a Goal or Set a Record

Let us not become weary in doing good, for at the proper time we will reap a harvest if we do not give up. Galatians 6:9

Years ago on a balmy Sunday afternoon, Lawrence Mc-Cutcheon of the Los Angeles Rams football team broke what at the time had been the record for total yards gained as a Ram player. He did it in five years. The record had been established by Dick Bass, who took nine years to set it. On the same day, McCutcheon broke loose for a forty-eight yard run, and radio announcers informed the listening world that it was the longest run of his career.

An exercise in arithmetic is helpful here. Add one fact to the other, and you come to a remarkable conclusion. The record number of total yards plus no single run over forty-eight yards adds up to the deduction that records are set and goals are achieved with over and over, again and again, grind-it-out-one-step-at-a-time, hard, hot, monotonous work.

We set our goals and suppose they are reached and new records are established in memorable moments and on grand occasions. We imagine that our more impressive accomplishments are inevitably accompanied by a full symphony orchestra or punctuated with a standing ovation by an appreciative audience. Sorry! It just doesn't work that way. What is accomplished in this life, particularly in the sphere of church or congregational service, is far more likely achieved at a pedestrian pace by hard work, perspiration, and drudgery. The only time the music begins is when God puts what you do and I do and everybody else does all together, and all that daily routine and slogging it out step by step becomes the march of the church in triumph.

Think how Solomon's temple was originally built (1 Kings 5:13–18). For years minimum-wage day laborers tramped off into the forests of old Lebanon and hacked away, day after miserable day, with the primitive instruments of the times, until at last some ancient cedar gave way and came down. And then it was on to the next tree and the next. It was bitter work, useless as far as anyone could tell, all drudgery, until after seven years (1 Kings 6:38) they all trooped down to Jerusalem—stone carvers, wood whittlers, clean-up people— and there they saw the temple that their efforts had created.

When the temple was finished and the ark of the Lord was brought to it, they sacrificed "so many sheep and cattle that they could not be recorded or counted" (1 Kings 8:5). Then the celebration began. These words are simply too suggestive of a most pertinent notion to let them pass unused. The burnt offering, given our context, stands for the sacrifices you make over each long day, the untold hours and the never noticed, sometimes painful contribution you make back in the shadows. God has sent some of you into the forests of old Lebanon, some of you into the quarries, and some of you down into the salt mines where you labor, forgotten and, it seems, forever. "Life," someone has said, "is so daily." Isn't that the truth?

Isaiah had a pretty good handle on how it works: "They will soar on wings like eagles; they will run and not grow weary, they will walk and not be faint" (40:31). A soaring flight, yes; a heavenly dash, you bet; but must it slow down to a walk?

However, prizes are won at a walk, in the third mile. Count the hours of your life and see. Very little of our work week is spent in soaring flight or headlong dashes. Mostly you walk. Most of your days your feet hit the floor at the same hour, you eat the same breakfast, take the same street to the office, deal with the same people, meet the same problems, and face the same responsibilities. You don't need instructions to know

how to fly. You don't require special training to run. You
need something or someone to help you walk, someone to
assist with the daily grind, the plodding of life, a companion
for the routine, a power for the ordinary day, something to
help you "walk and not be faint."

And to bring that home to us is the story of one who was
born in a barn, wrapped in swaddling clothes, and laid in a
manger. Thirty years he spent around his father's carpenter
shop. Even then it wasn't a victory to be had at a single stroke.
Three more years while his relatives shrugged their shoulders
and rolled their eyes. His friends dropped off one by one until
at last he stood alone on the far side of the cross. Such a long
road with all those years and the pain and the dying. That's
how he won the salvation of the world.

Have you got it—power to plod on and a way to walk,
to reach your goals and set your records? Jesus can infuse
into our ordinary days the power to do a day's work and
enthusiasm for the same old tasks, if he can only set up shop
in our hearts. He can be a light for your path and a lamp for
your way, all day, every day. Isaiah looked into the future and
saw Jesus in it. "Oh my," he declared, "just see what happens
now. People are going to soar on wings as eagles. They will
run and not grow weary. But, best of all, praise God, watch
how they will walk and not be faint."

Chances are tomorrow is just another day for you. But
were you to place your hand in the hand of the man called
Jesus, think what it could be. It could be one more leg in the
achievement of a great goal, one more step toward a record.
The little tasks which comprise your ministry don't have to
be the same old little tasks at all, but part of your walk with
Jesus. As your daily rounds begin, praise God for each fellow
striver, for your health if you have it, for the glory of another
day in the great walk of life. When the snags and jolts show
up, see them in perspective alongside the strides you are
making toward your goal. And when tomorrow is over, take
its defects and worries and leave them all behind. Add one
more segment, one more leg. That's how records are set.

It's a long walk to eternity. A person can get tired. No one can walk that far unless Jesus walks alongside. But with him, when the daily walk and sacrifice begins, so does the celebration.

For Group or Personal Reflection

1. As regards the church's work of ministry, who should get the glory?
2. What is the difference between giving glory and affirmation?
3. When do you tend to wear out?
4. How are you personally rejuvenated?
5. How does Jesus walk with you?

To Take This One Step Farther

1. Read Deut. 5:32; Josh. 1:7; and Prov. 4:27. What suggestions do these passages make to you for your daily grind?
2. Read Phil. 3:13. What is Paul's secret for coping with the long haul?
3. Set your goals for a year. Increment by quarters where you aspire to be on your way to that goal. Set aside a day each three months to assess your progress, to reorder your calendar, or to celebrate your success.

Prayer

O God, my God, I cannot go forth unless you go with me. Keep me from relying on my strength and teach me to walk with my hand firmly in yours. Then lead me, step by deliberate step, along the paths of righteousness, until I come safely home. Amen.

Chapter 16

The Gospel of Another Chance

Who is a God like you, who pardons sin and forgives the transgression ...? You do not stay angry forever but delight to show mercy. You will again have compassion on us; you will tread our sins underfoot and hurl all our iniquities into the depths of the sea. Micah 7:18–19

Ours is the gospel of another chance. Always. You don't ever come to the end of God's love. You never encounter a line in the sand and God on the other side declaring, "Thus far and no farther." Never, ever will you hear God say that. That's what it means when the poet rhapsodizes, "Every morning mercies new." It's always a fresh beginning, the opportunity to "start from scratch," another chance.

That is a most practical and reassuring word at the end of the day, when all there is to look back on is the way you have botched it once again. The staff leader, the chairman of the board, the whole membership of the PTA, and the senior pastor—all may be clucking and fretting and laying the blame at your door sill. But the real boss, the one for whom you really work, assures you, "Tomorrow is another day. We'll give it a go again in the morning. You'll have your try at it once more after a good night's sleep. We've got this gospel between us, you and I, the gospel of another chance."

That's the best news there is and for good reason. For one thing there is this first-hand knowledge each of us has of himself. If others are inclined to think poorly of you and your efforts, what would they think if they really knew—knew what

85

you know? There is nothing more devastating than to have to live with our mistakes or, even worse, our weaknesses. We don't allow ourselves the same space for failure we suffer others.

When we fold before the temptation of world and flesh, we struggle with our guilt through the sleepless night and bend under the burden of self-reproachment. We toss on our beds and roll over from side to side endlessly, hour after hour, trying to get away from the memory of secret sin, but when we unclench our eyes the enormity of our blunders and indulgences are right there, outlined against the wall, on that side of the bed too, accusing us. Where can you go to get away?

King David felt it in his bones and wept bitterly the whole night through (Ps. 6:6; 32:3). But then Christian memory, like one of Shakespeare's "angels and ministers of grace," working quite independent of your will, recalls the gospel of another chance. The patience of Job pales alongside the long-suffering mercy of our God (James 5:11).

Another reason this is such good news is that nothing else works. This yanking at the bootstraps simply makes matters worse. For one thing, by the time you get started it's already too late. The error, the "goof," the outright iniquity, is already there. No sense fixing your hope on what has already failed, namely, you. It is startling to discover how much of the average person's religion is still focused on what he can do and will do.

Another chance doesn't mean you start all over again. It means a new start, a new style, a new system with someone else at the wheel, in the driver's seat. This time the active agent is Christ and the power is God's. If you slip once more because you insist on getting your hands into it, you can start all over again with the great ONE taking over—again and again and again.

That's the gospel, but the good news is it's yours. It's not just a proclamation you have been commissioned to preach or teach or share or demonstrate. It's a gospel that rescues

you, and because of it you can "lay me down to sleep." Ours
is the gospel of another chance, this time with Christ in you
doing the doing, to do his will "on earth and make his kingdom
come."

What a great gospel there is at the heart of every Christian
life—church workers' lives too! There is no disfunction in
your behavior that cannot be made over by God's hands into
what he wills. There is no thorn in your week which cannot
be woven into a crown. There is no disharmony which cannot
become glorious music when he gets hold of it. And what
God has done and does each day for you, he does with the
work of your hands as well.

Those work-related dreams of yours, those fond hopes—
when they all get shattered or derailed, that's not the end of
the story. When your best efforts and the plans so painstak-
ingly drawn, the aims and goals so nobly set and carefully
crafted, are blown out of the water (often by some careless,
off-hand remark on the part of somebody who lives out on
the periphery and neither understands nor has shared the
agony by which the plans came into being) that's not the end.
Don't throw up your hands in disgust and despair.

Smile. Learn what there is to be learned. Amend what
there is to amend. But inside, where no one can see and no
one can hear, remind yourself, "All right, but I have something
going for me of which you may be unaware. On my side there
is always another chance. My whole ministry is in the service
of the gospel of another chance. That's my secret weapon in
this holy war. That's where this funny grin comes from. I know
something you might not. En garde! Here we go again."

There is something to be said for not giving up. You hav-
en't come close to the end of God's rope, and you never will.
Consider the long haul. Christian ministry and service may
scale a mountain here and there and have lofty moments, but
mostly it's a matter of foot before foot across the endless
flatland. It's a matter of slogging it out. For such a trek, for
the likes of us, nothing is more practical and nothing is more
glorious than the news, the gospel, of another chance.

For Group or Personal Reflection

1. How much do you personally struggle with the "gospel of another chance"?
2. How can you best communicate the gospel of another chance to others?
3. How can the gospel of another chance fit in with constructive criticism and accountability?
4. How much of your religion is focused on what you can do and will do?
5. Is there a danger that belief in a gospel of another chance can lead to what Dietrich Bonhoeffer calls "cheap grace"? (Cheap grace is forgiveness as a principle for living apart from the costly cross of Christ, and apart from the costly repentance and fruits of repentance on our part.) If so, how can that danger be avoided?

To Take This One Step Farther

1. Give yourself a moment to recall and then name two heroes from the Old Testament and two from the New Testament whose contribution to the kingdom of God would never have occurred were it not for the gospel of another chance.
2. Thank God in specific terms for the times he has afforded you a second chance. First he forgives; then he remakes; and then he uses you again.

Prayer

O God, great and glorious, whose mercy waits patiently for those who return with penitent hearts, I praise you that every day brings with it a brand new opportunity. The past is over, and you have forgiven all that I did wrong. The future waits for the story that my life writes. Let what I do and say praise you, since you have given to us all the miracle of still another chance. Amen.

Chapter 17

Just One More Thing

Serve wholeheartedly, as if you were serving the Lord, not men, because you know that the Lord will reward everyone for whatever good he does. Eph. 6:7–8

Have you ever asked yourself, "If I had only one more opportunity to say something—anything—to those I serve, what would it be?" The fascination is how the answer to that question changes from day to day. Last week it's one thing, tomorrow quite another.

It's the same thing now, in conclusion to this series of essays. One more thing to say; one more chance to say it; what will it be? If it weren't for book editors and deadlines, these things might never end. Like the horizon the end keeps pressing back. Ah yes, just one more thing and then you're off again.

So what is printed here, in conclusion, really isn't final. It's just what comes to mind today. Tomorrow would be something else. See? That's a good idea for a different kind of ending. If we had the luxury to follow our inclinations, we could add another chapter and name it "Tomorrow Will Be Something Else Again." After that would doubtless come another; then another. But we are committed now, and we'll stick with it. There is just one more thing to say, and then we'll let it go at that. We've chosen three key words in conclusion: priorities, perspective, and praise.

People, at least some of them, think they choose priorities. They don't, of course. They demonstrate them. Priorities are so often thrust on people by environment, by outside factors, even by heredity. Watch people long enough and you'll likely be able to list their priorities, catalogue them in the order of their perceived importance.

For one person, work comes first, for another, family. Health, says this one. That one says reputation. All of the above, maybe, except what is really inviolate, what may not be interfered with, what is a rule of life: is the Monday morning golf game. Arguments in defense of that priority are established early on and offered inevitably, even when no one is asking for them.

What is your #1 priority? When people observe you through the whole day, keep an eye on you for a month, what do they see about what comes first with you? Well, God comes first. He is preeminent. Is he? Is he first; does he take prior place in your life? God has his rival. That rival is you. When all is said and done, the conflicts in life boil down to this: who's on first; who comes first; who's got first place—you or your Lord? Priorities. They are set for you by the big priority—God first and last and always. And the only thing that stands in the way is you.

Perspective is next. Homespun philosophy is almost always the best kind. Here is a piece of it: Ask yourself, "What difference will it make twenty years from now?" One way to get at that is to look back twenty years and determine what was happening in your life then that has truly mattered. How quickly and easily you can slough off those monumental battles over acoustical tile in the youth room as opposed to a hard surface ceiling, or a new Sunday School bus versus repaving the parking lot. At the time, of course, the arguments possessed—even obsessed—your waking hours, and played total havoc with a full night's rest.

Relationships were destroyed and people left the church, bitter because their points of view were passed over unheeded. Now, twenty years later, what difference did it make? Not enough, I'd wager, to warrant the unhappiness and the disjuncture it produced. The only difference anything makes in twenty years is the difference it makes in someone. Something doesn't matter; someone does.

A vicar or intern you trained is a fine, effective pastor today, twenty years later. That matters. A teenager to whom you conveyed the most basic Christian principles shines now as a paragon of moral strength and piety in the business world, where piety and inner strength are rare. That matters. A baby baptized, a youngster listened to, a divorcing person supported, a congregation served—these make a difference twenty years from now. Twenty years from now what matters is what you have done to, what you have done for, someone. Perspective.

And praise. "Praise and thanksgiving," the hymn begins. "Praise and thanksgiving," that's how we end. It's not just our duty, though God calls for it over and over again (Ps. 66:2; John 9:24). It's not only our privilege, even though it is that. Oh, it is that (Heb. 13:15). Mostly it is effervescence, a bubbling up inside which cannot be contained, up and over until it splashes around you where no one can miss it and everyone is affected by it. Thank God. Praise God. "Give thanks to the Lord," not because things are good. They aren't not always, not usually. "Give thanks to the Lord for HE is good; his mercy endures forever" (Ps. 106:1).

That is, when all is said and done, the great, overriding secret to this business of serving in the church: God's goodness, to you, for you, through you. That's why church workers need constantly to stand before their God in earnest prayer; need to read and ponder his Word and will each day; and need to renew their strength at the Holy Table with regularity. Without a full, daily dose of the love of God, sustained labor in the church is quite beyond us. With a full boost each day from the God who is love, church work is well within the ability of us all. It is God who sets our priorities, who provides us with perspective, and who prompts our words and works of praise. Those are words a church worker might well live by.

For Group or Personal Reflection

1. If you had only one more opportunity to say something to those you serve, what would it be?

2. What are your "lived out" priorities?
3. What are you doing now that will matter twenty years from now?
4. How can you yourself best praise and thank God in Christ?
5. What is one last thing you would like to say to the others in your group?

To Take This One Step Farther

Count your special blessings, you servant of the great and triune God. Name them one by one. Get started. It will require the rest of your life even to make a good beginning.

Prayer

> Spirit of the holy God, grant that none of what I know about your holy Word and will, and nothing of what you have taught me about your love and mercy, may be left behind by me or forgotten as I turn again to my cycle of common tasks. Enable me to bring my will into harmony with yours, so that I may serve in peace, do your will on earth, and see your kingdom come. Amen.